curious about

TIE-DOWN ROPING

BY RACHEL GRACK

AMICUS LEARNING

What are you

curious about?

Curious About is published by
Amicus Learning, an imprint of Amicus
P.O. Box 227, Mankato, MN 56002
www.amicuspublishing.us

Editor: Ana Brauer
Series Designer: Kathleen Petelinsek
Book Designer and Photo Researcher: Kathleen Petelinsek

Library of Congress Cataloging-in-Publication Data
Names: Koestler-Grack, Rachel A., 1973– author.
Title: Curious about tie-down roping / by Rachel Grack.
Description: Mankato, MN : Curious About is published by Amicus Learning, [2025] | Series: Curious about Rodeo | Includes bibliographical references and index. | Audience: Ages 6–9 years | Audience: Grades 2–3 | Summary: "Learn how cowboys and their horses compete in tie-down roping events in this question-and-answer book for elementary-aged readers. Includes infographics and back matter to support research skills along with a table of contents, glossary, books and websites for further research, and an index"—Provided by publisher.
Identifiers: LCCN 2024015021 (print) | LCCN 2024015022 (ebook) | ISBN 9798892000901 (lib bdg) | ISBN 9798892001489 (paperback) | ISBN 9798892002066 (ebook)
Subjects: LCSH: Calf roping—Juvenile literature.
Classification: LCC GV1834.45.C34 K646 2025 (print) | LCC GV1834.45.C34 (ebook) | DDC 791.8/4—dc23/eng/20240508
LC record available at https://lccn.loc.gov/2024015021
LC ebook record available at https://lccn.loc.gov/2024015022

Photo Credits: Alamy Stock Photo/Cowboy and Western, 11 (top), Luc Novovitch, 12–13, Mauro Toccaceli, cover, 1, 6–7, Nyla James, 10, Robert McGouey, 3, 20–21, Yaroslav Sabitov/YES Market Media, 8-9; Shutterstock/Diane Garcia, 2 (left), 5, digitmilk, 17, 22, 23, Jackson Stock Photography, 11 (bottom left), 11 (bottom right), 18–19, Jim Lambert, 11 (bottom middle), Macrovector, 17, satriana, 17, YES Market Media, 2 (right), 15

Printed in China

CHAPTER ONE

What is tie-down roping?

It's a timed rodeo event. A cowboy on horseback chases down a calf. He tosses a lasso around its neck and jumps off his horse. He throws the calf down on the ground. He quickly ties together three of its legs. Cowboys compete to see who is fastest!

DID YOU KNOW?
Tie-down roping is a men's event at most professional rodeos. Ladies compete at women's rodeos and nonsanctioned events.

Tie-down roping is also called calf roping.

Why rope a calf?

Calf roping started on ranches in the Old West. Now, it is one of the most popular rodeo sports.

It was a common ranch chore years ago. Sometimes calves got sick or hurt. The only way to catch them was by roping them. This held it still for vet care. Every cowboy tried to be the fastest to rope and tie. Roping became a competition.

CHAPTER TWO

2

When does the clock start?

If the roper doesn't give the calf a head start, he breaks the barrier and gets a penalty.

The action starts before the clock does. The **chute** opens and the calf runs into the arena. It gets a head start. A rope tied around its neck pulls tight and falls off. The **barrier rope** drops, and the clock starts. The roper blasts out of the **box**. The chase is on!

DID YOU KNOW?
Tie-down roping is "catch as catch can." This means any catch is allowed.

Is the calf hard to catch?

Even young kids can learn to throw a lasso.

Yes! Roping on horseback takes lots of practice. The cowboy must time his throw just right. And he needs both hands free. He cannot use the reins to command his horse. But that's okay. His horse is well trained. It knows what to do.

Beginners compete in dummy roping. This is a great way to start roping!

TIE-DOWN TALK

Top notch: the rope catches the top of the head

Trash in the loop: legs caught in the rope

Bell collar catch: a clean catch around the neck

How do ropers train their horses?

This cowboy practices his roping skills using a mechanical calf.

DID YOU KNOW?
Ropers often practice with a heavy log instead of a live calf. This allows the horse to work on each step at a slower pace.

Ropers practice with their horses every day. They work together as a team. The horse learns to follow the roper's body movements. It stops as soon as he throws the rope. But then the roper must dismount. He teaches the horse to back up and tighten the rope alone.

What is in the roper's mouth?

That's a **pigging string**. Ropers use it to tie down the calf. They carry it between their teeth. The roper runs to the calf and throws it down. He gathers three legs together. He grabs the pigging string to tie them up. He makes two wraps and a **hooey**. He throws his arms in the air. Time!

DID YOU KNOW?

The horse holds the rope tight. But it knows not to pull too hard. The calf must stay on its feet. If it falls, ropers must let it get up before throwing it down. This costs valuable time.

The cowboy holds the rope in his mouth so his hands are free to throw down the steer.

Does the calf get hurt?

It could. But rodeos have rules to keep calves safe. Ropers only get 25 seconds to rope and tie. Calves must be picked up and flipped on their side. No **jerk downs** are allowed. That's when the calf gets pulled onto its back or head. Ropers who break the rules get a "no time."

DID YOU KNOW?
The Professional Rodeo Cowboys Association (PRCA) has over 60 rules about proper care and treatment of the animals.

1. **SAFETY WEIGHT:**
   215 POUNDS (98 KG) –
   285 POUNDS (129 KG)

2. **HEALTHY AND FIT**

3. **25-SECOND TIME LIMIT**

4. **NO JERK DOWNS**

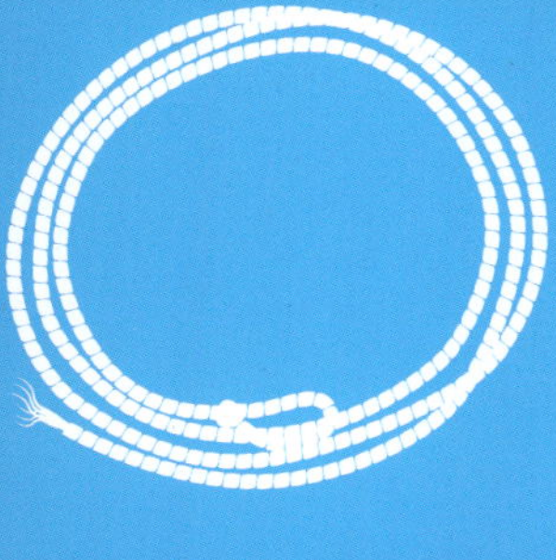

5. **CATCH ROPE QUICKLY REMOVED FROM NECK**

CHAPTER THREE

What is a "no time"?

It means the roper got disqualified. Maybe he broke a rule. Or the calf kicked free. It must stay tied for six seconds. The roper climbs back on his horse. They step forward to give the neck rope some **slack**. If the calf breaks loose, the time does not count.

Sometimes the calf breaks free before the roper is done. Then the roper is disqualified.

The world record for tie-down roping is 6.3 seconds.

Who wins?

The roper with the fastest time. But he also needs a clean run. Maybe a roper got the calf tied down in seven seconds. But he broke the barrier. This means he left the box too soon. Uh-oh. He gets a 10-second **penalty**. That puts him out of the money this **go-round**!

STAY CURIOUS

ASK MORE QUESTIONS

Where can I learn to rope?

Are there rodeos near me?

Try a BIG QUESTION: Would I feel bad roping a calf?

SEARCH FOR ANSWERS

Search the library catalog or the Internet.
A librarian, teacher, or parent can help you.

Using Keywords
Find the looking glass.

Keywords are the most important words in your question.

If you want to know:

- about roping classes near you, type: YOUTH ROPING [YOUR CITY/STATE]
- about rodeos nearby, type: RODEOS IN [YOUR STATE]

FIND GOOD SOURCES

Here are some good, safe sources you can use in your research.
Your librarian can help you find more.

Books

Breakaway Roping
by Rachel Grack, 2025.

Tie-Down Roping
by Rochelle Groskreutz, 2020.

Internet Sites

Britannica: Calf Roping
https://www.britannica.com/sports/calf-roping
Britannica is an encyclopedia with educational information on many topics. Learn more about calf roping.

Kiddle: Calf Roping
https://kids.kiddle.co/Calf_roping
Kiddle is an online encyclopedia for kids. Search for information on a wide variety of educational topics.

SHARE AND TAKE ACTION

Watch tie-down roping.
Ask an adult to help you find videos of tie-down roping events.

Take horseback riding classes.
You need excellent riding skills to rope!

Rope a dummy.
Take a roping class and see if you like it.

GLOSSARY

barrier rope A rope that hangs across the front of the box barrier.

box The pen where riders back their horses into for a timed rodeo event.

chute The pen that holds animals in position so the riders can safely mount.

go-round A round of competition at the rodeo; most rodeos have more than one round.

hooey The knot used to finish tying the pigging string.

jerk down To flip a calf over backwards so it lands on its back with its feet in the air.

nonsanctioned Not approved or run by an official organization.

penalty A mark that counts against a score.

pigging string The rope used to tie the calf's legs together.

slack The loose part of a hanging rope.

INDEX

About the Author

Rachel Grack has been writing children's nonfiction for twenty-five years. She lives on a ranch in the heart of rodeo country (southern Arizona). Some evenings, she wanders over to watch her neighbors in friendly roping competitions. A western restaurant in town offers weekly bull riding and mutton busting. But Rachel much prefers a quiet ride on her gentle paint horse, Lady.